Series consultant: Dr Dorothy Rowe

The author and publisher would like to thank the staff and pupils of the following schools for their help in making this book: St Barnabas Church of England Primary School, Pimlico; Kenmont Primary School, Hammersmith & Fulham; St Vincent de Paul Roman Catholic School, Westminster; Mayfield Primary School, Cambridge; St Peter's Church of England Primary School, Sible Hedingham.

A CIP catalogue record for this book is available from the British Library.

ISBN 978-0-7136-6076-0

Reprinted 2003, 2004, 2009
First paperback edition published 2002
First published in hardback in 1997 by
A & C Black Publishers Ltd,
36 Soho Square, London, W1D 3QY www.acblack.com

This book is produced using paper that is made from wood grown in managed, sustainable forests. It is natural, renewable and recyclable. The logging and manufacturing processes conform to the environmental regulations of the country of origin.

Printed in China through Colorcraft Ltd., Hong Kong.

CHOICES

Telling the Truth

Althea

Photographs by Charlie Best

Illustrations by Conny Jude

A & C Black · London

What is telling the truth?

When you describe what you know has happened, or something that you really think or feel, that is telling the truth. If you pretend that something did happen when it didn't, or say something which you don't really believe, then you are telling a lie.

Why do you think we should tell the truth?

If you tell a lie once, next time they don't believe you.

You don't get in as much trouble as you do if you lie.
Lying makes you feel guilty.

Everyone tells lies at some time or another.
Can you think of any occasions when
it's alright to tell a lie?

Ryan says, "Mum told a lie the
other day. She said we couldn't
go to lunch with her friend,
as we had already been
asked out that day.
It was really because
me and my brother
don't like the
children, so it's
better if Mum goes
on her own.

I think that was
a good lie:
it didn't hurt
anyone."

People sometimes tell very small lies,
so as not to hurt other people's feelings.
These lies are called white lies or fibs.

I told Hannah I liked her shoes, although I didn't really, because she was feeling miserable about them. She had to wear the shoes out to a party anyway, so why not make her feel better about them?

Sherri remembers, "When Mum bought a new dress, she asked me if I liked it. I said I liked the colour. I didn't tell her it made her look fat. I suppose I avoided telling a lie!"

Dad was planning a surprise party for Mum, and we had to lie a bit so she wouldn't know about it. We hid her presents too.

Sometimes, keeping a secret might mean telling lies. If it's a good secret, which no one can be hurt by, it's all right not to tell the whole truth.

Tanice remembers, 'When my brother asked me what Mum and Dad were giving him for his birthday, I lied and said I didn't know.'

When it feels wrong to lie, you shouldn't do it. If someone asks you to keep a secret, and you don't think it's a good secret, then you should tell the truth, even though it might get both of you into trouble.

How does it make you feel when you tell lies to get yourself out of trouble?

Nada says, "I feel very guilty when I tell a lie. Once I was so sick that Mum had to put me to bed. She couldn't understand what was wrong with me. She was going to ring the doctor, so I had to tell her about the lie. Now, when I'm feeling ill, she asks me lots of questions!"

Sometimes, other people may ask you to lie, to stop them getting into trouble.

Paul asked me not to tell when some of them stole sweets from the shop. It was too big a lie for me to keep, so I told my mum, and we talked about it.

Bullies can make you lie sometimes. They say they'll pick on you even more if you tell anyone what they're doing.

You may feel scared, but you have to try to pluck up courage and tell the truth. Tell your parents or a teacher, or an adult that you can trust. They should be able to help you sort it out.

11

People sometimes tell fibs to make themselves feel bigger and sound more important. They might exaggerate when they tell you about what has happened to them, or make up stories.

Once, when we were talking about pets, Paul said he had a pet giraffe! Everyone laughed - Paul was always telling those sort of stories to make people take notice of him.

When everyone knows a story is not true, it's sometimes called a tall story or make believe.

I told everyone I had peanut butter sandwiches, when I only had fish paste. It made me feel bigger, because they were all jealous!

Lies like these are silly, because the things you have or claim you have are not important. People like you for yourself, and not for what you have got. They may well like you less if you are always telling lies.

13

You may think that telling a small lie will get you out of trouble. But sometimes when you tell one lie, you have to tell another to cover it up, and you may end up in big trouble. Can you think of a time when this happened to you?

Peter told his mum he had done his homework, so he could watch TV. It was a lie - he hadn't learnt his words. When the teacher asked him the next day, he had to lie again and say he had forgotten to take the book home with him. His teacher called his mum after school, then Peter was in real trouble.

Mei says, "I copied my friend's sums, because I couldn't do them. Then the teacher gave me even more difficult sums to do, and I couldn't cope with them. In the end, I had to tell her I had copied my friend's work. She told me I was silly to cheat, because then she didn't know I needed help."

$$6 \times 5 = 30$$

People often won't believe you if they know you have lied about other things.

"We were playing in the playground, and someone kicked the ball onto the roof. Everyone ran away, and I got told off, even though it wasn't me."

When you tell the truth and people don't believe you, it feels very unfair.

Some adults may say you are lying, because they don't want what you said to be the truth.

After Dad left us, I told Mum I had seen him with Aunty Mo, but Mum said I was lying. I wasn't, I did see them.

It can be difficult to tell the truth when you know people are going to be cross with you.

Tanice says, "I knocked a plate off the shelf and it broke. I cleared up the pieces and put them in the dustbin. I wanted to tell Mum a lie, to say I didn't know anything about it. But in the end I plucked up courage and told her. She was very upset because she liked the plate. But I think she would have been a lot angrier if I hadn't told her."

Ella remembers,
"When I was playing,
I broke a chair.
I felt sick. I was
dreading telling Mum,
but she wasn't very cross.
She said these things
happen and she was
pleased I had told
the truth."

Sometimes you have
to be very brave to
tell the truth.

Adults sometimes tell you lies because they think that it is kinder to protect you from the truth. When something upsetting happens, adults often try to pretend nothing is wrong. Usually, you can tell something is wrong and you start to worry about it.

It's much easier to accept and understand what's going on, if people tell you the truth.

Mum was crying when I came in, so I knew Gran must be very ill. But she kept telling me that Gran would soon be better.

People can sometimes
make you lie to yourself.
They may want you
to be brave when
you don't feel like
being brave.

Maria tells herself
she's not angry
when really
she is, because
she's been told
nice girls don't
get angry.

Sherri tells herself that she doesn't miss her dad, when she's really very sad because her dad has gone away. She's been told that big girls don't cry.

It never helps to pretend to yourself that everything is alright when it's not. The only things you can ever know for certain are what goes on inside your own head - what you think and how you feel.

The most important person to be truthful with is yourself.

For teachers and parents

A note from Dorothy Rowe

Parents and teachers know that the demands of telling the truth can cause problems for children. But adults sometimes forget that in order to help, they must first find out how the child sees the problem. A child won't see the the situation in the same way as an adult, because no two people ever see things in exactly the same way.

Remembering this, the parent or teacher won't say to themselves, 'I know what is wrong with the child', but will explore possible reasons for the child's behaviour: for example, 'Is this child lying because he is afraid of the consequences if he tells the truth?' or, 'Is she lying out of loyalty to her friend?'.

It's possible to think up dozens of alternative reasons as answers to the question, 'Why does this child behave like this?'. Doing so helps the adult to ask better questions. However, the answer can only come from the child.

The importance of telling the truth is an issue that we have to face throughout life. Parents and teachers should be prepared to talk to children about their own difficulties and experiences in dealing with this issue, and not pretend to provide easy solutions to the problems and anxieties which children encounter in this area. This way the adult and the child can explore the dilemma together.

You could start a discussion about telling the truth by getting everyone involved in making a list of sample situations in which there is a choice between lying and being truthful. Then, with the children, write down against each example whether you think it's important or very important to tell the truth, or when it might be all right to tell a lie. Examples might include:

• Saying that you have cleaned your teeth when you haven't.

• Eating the last chocolate and pretending it wasn't you.

• Telling someone that you like their new haircut when you think it's awful.

• Being late home and saying that it's because you had to stay at school.

Compare your answers - it could lead to an interesting discussion!

Many of the issues can be discussed page by page when going through the book again, but the following points may lead to a useful discussion.

Page 2 You want people to be honest with you. If everyone lied all the time, we wouldn't know who we could trust.

Page 6 What other examples can you think of where telling the truth would mean spoiling a surprise or giving away a secret?

Page 11 Telling someone that you are being bullied can be very difficult to do. Sometimes it can help if a friend comes with you to give you courage and to back you up.

Page 12 Having confidence in yourself means that you don't need to make up stories to impress other people.

Page 15 Cheating at games or in lessons is like lying. It's not much fun to play with someone who cheats, and it can be hard to gain someone's trust again if they know you have cheated at things in the past.

Page 19 Accidents do happen. Sometimes, people become very cross because they are upset about what has been broken rather than being angry with you for breaking it.

Page 21 Grown-ups often tell children that something isn't going to hurt them, when it will: for example, a visit to the dentist. Perhaps the adult is afraid of telling the child the truth, knowing what they are going to have to face. However, knowing what is going to happen can give the child a chance to prepare for it, and so make the experience more bearable. It's usually much easier to cope with something if you know the truth about it.

Page 23
What about big boys?

People see and remember things in different ways. When different people describe the same event, their versions may vary, although each person may be telling the truth as they remember it. We all have preconceptions that may colour our interpretation of what has happened.

Further reading

Children may find it interesting and helpful to have a look at some of the following books which also deal with the subject of telling the truth.

Clare Bevan
Ask Me No Questions
(Puffin, 1993)

Lois Lowry
Anastasia, Absolutely
(HarperCollins, 1997)

Hazel Townson
Charlie the Champion Liar
(Mammoth, 1996)